Animal Bodies

WHOSE TEETH ARE THOSE?

By Mary Griffin

Gareth Stevens
PUBLISHING

Please visit our website, www.garethstevens.com. For a free color catalog of all our high-quality books, call toll free 1-800-542-2595 or fax 1-877-542-2596.

Library of Congress Cataloging-in-Publication Data

Names: Griffin, Mary, 1978- author.
Title: Whose teeth are those? / Mary Griffin.
Description: New York : Gareth Stevens Publishing, [2024] | Series: Animal bodies | Includes index.
Identifiers: LCCN 2022047257 (print) | LCCN 2022047258 (ebook) | ISBN 9781538286500 (library binding) | ISBN 9781538286494 (paperback) | ISBN 9781538286517 (ebook)
Subjects: LCSH: Teeth–Juvenile literature.
Classification: LCC QL858 .G75 2024 (print) | LCC QL858 (ebook) | DDC 591.4/4–dc23/eng/20221018
LC record available at https://lccn.loc.gov/2022047257
LC ebook record available at https://lccn.loc.gov/2022047258

Published in 2024 by
Gareth Stevens Publishing
2544 Clinton Street
Buffalo, NY 14224

Designer: Tanya Dellaccio Keeney
Editor: Therese M. Shea

Photo credits: Cover, p. 1 Amelie Koch/Shutterstock.com; p. 5 Alicia Chelini/Shutterstock.com; p. 7 Irina No/Shutterstock.com; pp. 9, 11 thka/Shutterstock.com; p. 13 Neale Cousland/ Shutterstock.com; pp. 15, 24 Ingrid Heres/Shutterstock.com; pp. 17, 19, 24 Mikhail Cheremkin/ Shutterstock.com; pp. 21, 23 Martin Prochazkacz/Shutterstock.com.

Printed in the United States of America

CPSIA compliance information: Batch #CSGS24: For further information contact Gareth Stevens, at 1-800-542-2595.

Find us on

Contents

Let's look at animal teeth!
Look at these pointy teeth.

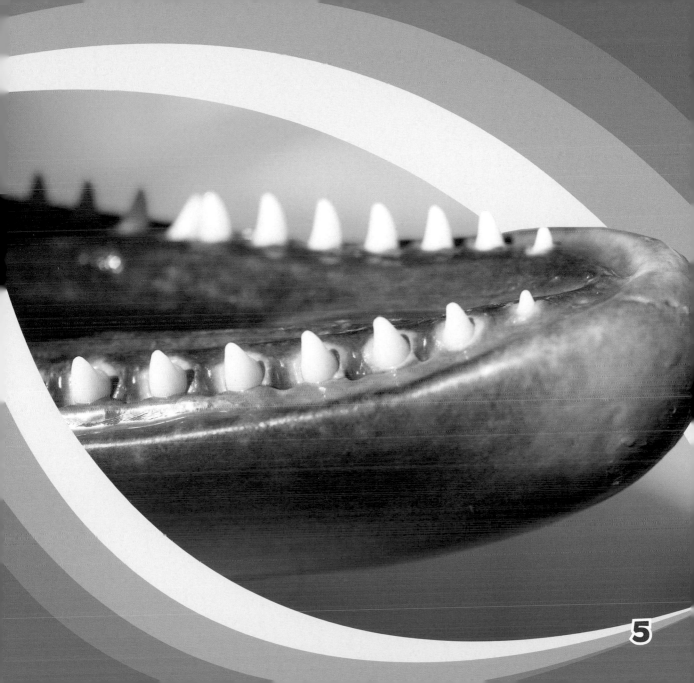

It's a dolphin!
Its teeth can grab fish.

Look at these little teeth.

It's a puppy!
Puppies lose their
first set of teeth.
They grow new teeth.

Look at these large teeth.

It's a hippo!
It fights with its teeth.

Look at these long teeth.

It's a walrus!
It uses its teeth to pull
itself onto land.

Look at these sharp teeth.

It's a great white shark!
It has about 300 teeth.

Words to Know

hippo

walrus

Index

24